One in the Chamber

At that time Mary got ready and hurried to a town in the hill country of Judea, where she entered Zechariah's home and greeted Elizabeth. When Elizabeth heard Mary's greeting, the baby leaped in her womb, and Elizabeth was filled with the Holy Spirit. In a loud voice she exclaimed: "Blessed are you among women, and blessed is the child you will bear! But why am I so favored, that the mother. NIV, Luke 1:39-44
Note: This was the first meeting of Jesus and John the Baptist. They would meet again when they were much older when John the Baptist baptizes him...

Imagine The Devil's Advocate meets the Passion of the Christ. Do you recall the scene of the dark shadowy figure lurking in crowd holding a baby in The Passion of the Christ? It was a profound and surreal scene.

It dawned on me that a baby is so fragile. It appeared Satan was not defeated and this time around he was going for the children…. he has evolved.

What if Mary had been convinced to have an ABORTION? One of the central characters in the snippet below unknowingly entered into a relationship with an organization affiliated with dark forces. This organization is intent upon eliminating the messiah and his prophets for generations via program shrouded in mystery and deceit.

א

A young lady enters the office of Doctor Evals.
The Doctor's countenance is stern. The lines in
his creased forehead tell the story. Gone are the
days when he was free to practice actual medicine.
Long before the mysterious gentlemen in the
bright white suit entered his small office in the
heart of downtown St. Maurice; population
1500...

A slight smile attacks the corner of his lips as he
recalls the offer he couldn't refuse. An
opportunity to save young mothers from
themselves, or so he thought.

Dr Evals had presented this scrip many times over
the last six years. The midway point of the
project. Many nights spent wondering how many
will experience the.... How many will sign?

Monday mornings come so fast.... and so it
begins.

Never fear Dear Sweet Mother, if you want the abortion, it can be accommodated.

Just sign right here. Yes, Right here on the bottom line. Thank you. You may leave now. You will be contacted…. Oh yeah! What is your phone number and address? Thanks.

In twelve years, you will be contacted on the child's birthday at which time you will be debriefed. We will tell you all about your child. We will keep the Birth Certificate on file.

We will invite you to the execution at which time you will be presented with a Death Certificate. Of Course this is yours to keep.

The death will be by execution one shot to the temple. We will not begin until you arrive. The child already knows you. There will be no need for introductions. He knew you in the womb. However your presence is required as we need a witness!

You will receive correspondence from this office once a year. This is the only time you will be contacted. You will receive update such as; The Child has a ferocious appetite for knowledge. The Child is progressing well in Science and the Arts. The Child loved birds etc...those types of things.

Dr Evals walks across the room and to the stained cedar cabinet with the stone granite door. It reminded him of a tomb. He opened the door with its multiple shelves containing all of the little silver boxes. Aimlessly, he reached into the cabinet and grabbed one. It did not matter which he chose, he knew the contents all too well.
Dr. Evals rubbed his left temple as there was suddenly a sharp pain there. One in the chamber..........

He presented her with the beautiful little ornate box. He then escorted her to the birthing area...

PLEASE SIGN
HERE_____

ב

Food for Thought

Note: The following definitions taken from Religioustolerance.org. Medical Definitions Author unknown

Human person: Any form of human life that is also considered a person, and thereby has civil rights, including the right to life. There is a societal consensus that a newborn is a human person. People disagree about whether a zygote, embryo, or fetus is a human person. People have different opinions about the stage at which human life becomes a human person. This is the core disagreement that drives the abortion wars

Barnabas: "You shall not kill either the fetus by abortion or the new born" (Letter of Barnabas, circa 125)

St. John Chrysostom (circa 340 - 407 CE): "Why sow where the ground makes it its care to destroy the fruit? Where there are many efforts at abortion? Where there is murder before the birth? For you do not even let the harlot remain a mere harlot, but make her a murderer also. You see how drunkenness leads to whoredom, whoredom to adultery, adultery to murder; or rather something even worse than murder. For I have no real name to give it, since it does not destroy the thing born but prevents its being born. Why then do you abuse the gift of God and fight with His laws, and follow after what is a curse as if a blessing, and make the place of procreation a chamber for murder, and arm the woman that was given for childbearing unto slaughter?" Homily 24 on Ro

A while back....

Mary is tossing and turning in bed. She has had a disturbing dream that has her very confused. In her dream the Angel of God appears to inform Mary she is having a baby... She awakens, her mine is racing. Is it a dream or reality? Did she imagine this?

Joseph has a similar experience concerning the birth of a son; and realizes it has disturbed him greatly.

Lucifer the prince of darkness is fully aware of the events; he is seething as he calculates his next move. How can he stop this Immaculate Conception? He must come up with a plan to end this now. The battle has begun.

He knows Mary must inform Joseph that she is with child. He feels he must get to Joseph...If only just a whisper in his ear he could plant the seed of distrust and resentment.

If only he or his minions could approach Mary and plant the seed of doubt and distrust. Tell her she is nothing; why would God choose her for such an important role. Tell her Joseph will never believe her…and then.

Recommend the procedure; recommend someone that can make it all go away. Befriend her; console her; and convince her. She should not have this child! Joseph will not believe you! You will be ridiculed! You will be shunned! Let her know that you are there to help her.

א

For Satan knows if he can crucify Jesus in the womb…..

Note: The following definitions taken from Religioustolerance.org. Medical Definitions Author unknown

Human life: This is any living entity that has DNA from the species homo sapiens.

This includes an ovum, spermatozoon, zygote, embryo, and fetus. It also includes an infant, child, adult, elder. It also includes a breast cancer cell and a hair follicle and a skin scraping. Some forms of human life have little or no value; others are the most valuable and precious form of life in the known universe.

Human person: Any form of human life that is also considered a person, and thereby has civil rights, including the right to life. There is a societal consensus that a newborn is a human person. People disagree about whether a zygote, embryo, or fetus is a human person. People have different opinions about the stage at which human life becomes a human person. This is the core disagreement that drives the abortion wars

How and so ever, if Satan was to be successful with Mary and Joseph that zygote, embryo, fetus that was to become Jesus, would not have been born. No lord and savior. No young man in the temple; nothing for Mathew, Mark, Luke and John to write about…

ז

The Birthing Area...

It is a very beautiful and ornate room. Extremely high ceilings, high backed chairs, all seeming to conceal the tools required for the transport of a child into this dimension.

Dr. Evals begin to explain the birthing process to Dear Sweet Mother as she glanced about the room. She asked in a somewhat uncertain voice? Are you sure you are going to pay me during the length of my pregnancy if I go through with this?

Of course Dear Sweet Mother you will be compensated and you will give birth. We have a contract. We will ensure everything goes according to plan.

Dr. Evals allowed his mind to wander to a passage he had read earlier that day and the unfortunate images he had been shown by the Prince of Darkness himself. He shivered.

Anon: writing circa 135 CE in The Apocalypse of Peter:

"I saw a gorge in which the discharge and excrement of the tortured ran down and became like a lake. There sat women, and the discharge came up to their throats; and opposite them sat many children, who were born prematurely, weeping. And from them went forth rays of fire and smote the women on the eyes. These were those who produced children outside of marriage, and who procured abortions." 26

Dr. Evals blinked in attempt to rid himself of the image. He then went on to reiterate that she would be compensated well as long as she adhered to the demands of the contract. She was ensured her abortion wish would be granted...unfortunately she believed him.

AT Twelve resounded repeatedly in Dr. Evals mind…..and another shiver.

And then…something that he remembers from long ago perhaps in Sunday school, in the far reaches of his mind like a flash and accompanied by a searing pain… just as quickly it was gone.

Now the word of the LORD came to me saying, "Before I formed you in the womb I knew you, and before you were born I consecrated you; I have appointed you a prophet to the nations." (NAS, Jeremiah 1:4-5)

I will say to God: … "Your hands shaped me and made me. Will you now turn and destroy me? Remember that you molded me like clay. Will you now turn me to dust again? (NIV, Job 10:2, 8-9)

ה

And now Dear Sweet Mother we are done. I will be in touch.

He knew the speech he would give her upon her return. He had delivered it so many times before…..

'

Baby Moses Laws:

Safe-haven laws (also known in some states as "Baby Moses laws") are statutes in the United States that decriminalize the leaving of unharmed infants with statutorily designated private persons so that the child becomes a ward of the state. "Safe-haven" laws typically let parents remain nameless to the court, often using a numbered bracelet system as the only means of linking the baby to the mother. Some states treat safe-haven surrenders as child dependency or abandonment, with a complaint being filed for such in juvenile court. The parent either defaults or answers the complaint. Others treat safe-haven surrenders as adoption surrenders, hence a waiver of parental rights (see parental responsibility). Police stations, hospitals, rescue squads, and fire houses are all typical locations to which the safe-haven law applies.[1]

Texas was the first state to enact a "Baby Moses Law" in 1999.[2]

I heard the King ordered death of firstborns under 2 years old in order to kill Moses…I'm just saying.

ה

The Bible: 'Life is sacred'   Remember Baby Malachi…. I'm just saying.

Human life is sacred because from its beginning it involves "the creative action of God." "Before I formed you in the womb I knew you, and before you were born I consecrated you" (Jer 1:5): The life of every individual, from its very beginning, is part of God's plan. Expressions of awe and wonder at God's intervention in the life of a child in its mother's womb occur again and again in the Psalms (for example, Ps 22:10-11; 71:6; 139:13-14).

The greatest destroyer of peace is abortion because if a mother can kill her own child, what is left for me to kill you and you to kill me? There is nothing between."…….Mother Theresa

I'm not naïve either…I'm just saying.

ש

Moloch, the Abomination of the Children of Ammon (excerpt)

Molech, whose name probably derived from Melech "king" and Bosheth, "shame", was one of the deities worshipped by the idolatrous Israelites. He was referred to as "the abomination of the children of Ammon" (1 Kings 11:7) and the primary means of worshipping him appears to be child sacrifice or "to pass through the fire." Solomon was said to have built a temple to him. "Then did Solomon build an high place for Chemosh, the abomination of Moab, in the hill that is before Jerusalem, and for Molech, the abomination of the children of Ammon." (1 Kings 11:7)

Sacrificing children was not uncommon, but the practice died down around the time of Jeremiah when the King defiled Tophet, the place where Moloch was worshipped.

"He also defiled Topheth, which is in the valley of the son of Hinnom, that no man might make his son or his daughter pass through the fire for Molech." (2 Kings 23:10)

"For the sons of Judah have done that which is evil in my sight,' declares the LORD, "they have set their detestable things in the house which is called by My name, to defile it. They have built the high places of Topheth, which is in the valley of the son of Hinnom, to burn their sons and their daughters in the fire, which I did not command, and it did not come into My mind. Therefore, behold, days are coming,' declares the LORD, "when it will no longer be called Topheth, or the valley of the son of Hinnom, but the valley of the Slaughter; for they will bury in Topheth because there is no other place." (Jer 7: 30-32)

Moloch has often been identified with Milcom, the god of the Ammonites. He was probably also identified with Baal, and as a sun or fire god, as he was also identified with the Assyrian/Babylonian

"Malik", and at Palmyra "Malach-bel". Moloch is also identified with Baal Hammon in Carthaginian religion.

Moloch was the god of the Ammonites, portrayed as a bronze statue with a calf's head adorned with a royal crown and seated on a throne. His arms were extended to receive the child victims sacrificed to him. Milton wrote that Moloch was a frightening and terrible demon covered with mothers' tears and children's blood.

Rabbis claim that in the famous statue of Moloch, there were seven kinds of cabinets. The first was for flour, the second for turtle doves, the third for an ewe, the fourth for a ram, the fifth for a calf, the sixth for a beef, and the seventh for a child. It is because of this, Moloch is associated with Mithras and his seven mysterious gates with seven chambers. When a child was sacrificed to Moloch, a fire was lit inside the statue. The priests would then beat loudly on drums and other objects so that the cries would not be heard.

'

Twelve Years Later...

Dr Evals welcomed Dear Sweet Mother...

He gave her the speech. He went to the tomb like cabinet and removed the tiny little box that had been assigned to her in their last meeting.

The box was placed in her hand and she was asked to open it and remove the contents. Dear sweet mother gasped as she removed the one silver bullet. She felt faint as her mind raced. What is going on? Why is there a bullet?

Dr Evals took the bullet from her palm and appeared to once again be escorting her to the birthing room. However; it was now very different, empty and cold. Why is it so cold in here she asked. Be quiet! The doctor's only response...

For the Dear Sweet Mother it all appeared to be in slow motion...The child was escorted into the room. The bullet was place into the gun. The gun was placed to the child's temple. The trigger pulled. The abortion carried out....the age of twelve.

Having said all of that...

Abortion can not be legislated; the object is not to submit women/couples to back alleys.

It is about educated choice.

A full understanding of what is at stake if an action is taken...............9 months * NO LIFE

A full understanding of what is at stake if no action is taken................9 months * LIFE

I'm not naïve...I'm just saying.

ל

How will we manage the unwanted?

How difficult is the adoption process?

What is the state of today's foster care system?

How do we factor in child abuse? How can it be avoided with unwanted children?

What programs exist today?

Healthcare challenges?

What is the role of the Church?

מ

Oh Yeah…..

Dear Sweet mother let out several primal screams. The gut wrenching wails reverberated within the chamber walls. Her child had been executed. However the mother child bond had not been severed. Dear Sweet Mother lunged forward to grasp the cloth the child was draped in to be carried away.

Dear Sweet Mother awakened drenched in sweat clawing at the sheets of her bed....

To be continued....

www.ingramcontent.com/pod-product-compliance
Lightning Source LLC
Chambersburg PA
CBHW030105300526
45785CB00019B/2776